HARRY HILL'S COLOSSAL COMPENDIUM

also by Harry Hill

A Complete History of Tim
Harry Hill's Whopping Great Joke Book
Harry Hill's Bumper Book of Bloopers

HARRY HILL'S
coLOSSaL
COMPENDIUM

BEST JOKES

**BEST
TIM
(the Tiny
Horse)**

**BEST
BLOOPERS**

FABER & FABER

First published in 2014
by Faber and Faber Limited
Bloomsbury House, 74-77 Great Russell Street,
London WCIB 3DA

Printed in the UK by CPI Group (UK) Ltd, Croydon, CRO 4YY
Design by Faber and Faber Ltd

A CIP record for this book
is available from the British Library

ISBN 978-0-571-31749-3
Typeset by Crow Books

FSC
www.fsc.org
MIX
Paper from
responsible sources
FSC® C101712

2 4 6 8 10 9 7 5 3 1

Dear Readers,

Welcome to this colossal, captivating, classy, compelling . . . er . . . calorific compendium, bursting at the seams with all my personal favourite jokes, bloopers and tales of Tim the Tiny Horse.

Feeling in the mood for a bite of romance? Where else can you find every joke, TV, magazine or newspaper goof AND Tim story about love that you could need all in one place? Nowhere, that's where! Or are you desperately looking for a snack of funny stories and one-liners about pets? Or celebrities? Or travel? They're all here at your fingertips! It's like a comedy vending machine! (See, I told you it was calorific!)

So empty the machine and scoff the lot by reading from cover to cover, or if you're just peckish, simply select what you're looking for and press the button (well, flick to the right page), and you'll soon have your friends – and yourself – in stitches.

Bon appetit, fellow comedians. Keep laughing!

Harry Hill

CONTENTS

Showbiz 9

Love and Romance 39

Travel 69

Families 101

Food 129

Weddings 169

Babies 195

Pets and Other Animals . . . 223

House and Home 259

Swimming and Other Things
   to Do in the Water 293

Celebrities 317

SHOWBIZ

Why was the unsuccessful magician hungry at break-time?
He'd forgotten his Twix.

Why did the hip-hop magician say that he hated amusements at Brighton?
He wanted to diss a pier.

I've just been beach fishing with the actors from the panto, but I couldn't get my bait out far enough to catch any big ones.
Feeble, useless cast?
Well, they're not exactly 'West End'.

Why did the actor put mustard on his ham?
He wanted to try a more challenging roll.

HARRY: My brother's with the circus – he gets £500 a week for swallowing a four-foot sword.
ALAN: What's so good about swallowing a four-foot sword?
HARRY: He's only three feet tall.

HARRY: I do like *Coronation Street* and the actress who played Bet Lynch. What's her real name – Julie . . .? Julie . . .?
ALAN: Goodyear!
HARRY: Not bad, but I'm looking forward to Christmas.

When I was a kid we didn't have a television, so my dad bored a hole through the wall into the house next door and we used to watch the wrestling every night – till we discovered that the neighbours didn't have a television either.

I did my first television show a year ago and the very next day one million television sets were sold. And the people who couldn't sell theirs threw them away.

I watched a very thought-provoking programme on television last night. The thought it provoked was, 'Why am I watching this programme?'

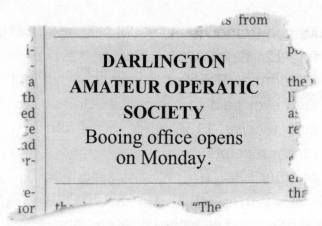

**DARLINGTON
AMATEUR OPERATIC
SOCIETY**
Booing office opens
on Monday.

Darlington and Stockton Times

Marlon Brando is being paid £2,250,000 for 12 days' work in the new film, Superman. Believed to be the highest sum ever paid to a film star, Brando will also receive 11.3 per cent of the box office receipts, which should give him another £3.

Manchester Evening News

6.10pm: Pride and Prejudice

Mr. Bennett's estranged cousin, Mr Collins, writes to announce his imminent visit to Longbourne – the house he will inherit on Mr Bennett's death. Mrs Bennett rallies the residents to stop him setting up a minicab service.

tim gets the showbiz bug

Tim the Tiny Horse was _so_ small that the blacksmith had to make his shoes from paperclips.

His saddle was made from
a watch-strap.

Which is why he never
wore it. Well, would you?

He was small... but he
had <u>Standards</u>.

Most of his activities were
severely restricted. So he
spent much of his time lazing
in the sun.

Or watching the TV.

One day Tim the Tiny Horse sat on the Patio watching the ants going about their business...

He admired their
sense of purpose.

'I need to get a job,'
he thought,

That lunchtime, as Tim sat
watching Anna Ford...

On the One O'Clock
News from the BBC,

he realised that
everyone on TV was
small... just like him.

It was perfect
for him!

Maybe he could be in a
cowboy film...

Or the Horse of the Year
Show...

or even read the Lunchtime
News with Anna!

Maybe he'd meet that
special lady horse
he'd always been looking for.

He knew he shouldn't get
his hopes up as from
what he'd seen, most
of the shows on TV
were set in pubs...

and he didn't like
pubs because often
there was a dog in
there.

If There was one thing Tim didn't like it was **DOGS**.

Without further ado
Tim the Tiny Horse
set off for the TV studio.

When he arrived at the studio
everything was much bigger than
he'd been led to believe.
In fact, everything was pretty
much full size.

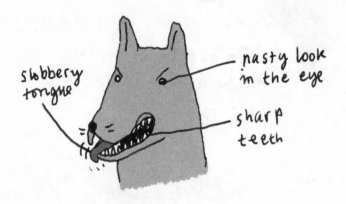

slobbery
tongue

nasty look
in the eye

sharp
teeth

Including the dog.

'I'm not sure I want
to be a part of this,'
he thought.

And instead headed off
to the canteen...

for a sugar lump.

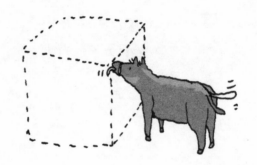

'Hmm...' thought Tim the Tiny Horse.
'The studios may not be what
I'd hoped... but the food
is first rate.'

With that, he headed for home.

After all...

there's no point in
getting a job for the
sake of it.

LOVE AND ROMANCE

Harry took his friend Steve home for dinner one evening and was greeted at the door by his wife, who flung her arms round him and kissed him passionately.

'That's amazing,' said Steve. 'You've been married all these years and yet your wife still welcomes you home like that.'

'Don't be fooled,' said Harry. 'She only does it to make the dog jealous.'

When people ask me the secret of our long marriage, I tell them. Twice a week we take time off to go this romantic little restaurant we know. There's dinner by candlelight, soft music and dancing under the stars.

She goes on Mondays and I go on Thursdays.

Every morning I take my wife her tea in my pyjamas. She loves it, but my pyjamas are getting a bit soggy.

ALAN: When I grow up, I'm going to marry the girl next door.
HARRY: Lovely! Do you fancy her, then?
ALAN: Not really, but I'm not allowed to cross the road.

The bad news is that my new girlfriend has terrible buck teeth. But the good news is that every time we kiss, she combs my moustache.

What did the envelope say to the stamp?
'Stick with me, baby, and we'll go places!'

HARRY: Doctor, doctor, can you take my tonsils out?
DOCTOR: Certainly. Would they prefer the zoo or the cinema?

Would you mind removing your tonsils, I can't see

Who is Dracula most likely to fall in love with?
The girl necks door.

How do vampires kiss?
Very carefully.

She was amazing! That girl had everything a man could want: big muscles, a beard, a moustache . . .

HARRY: Does your teacher like you?
LEON: Yes, she keeps putting kisses on my homework.

Will you love me when I'm old and wrinkled?
Of course I do.

HARRY: I'm afraid my dancing's not so good. I'm a little stiff from badminton.
WOMAN: I don't care where you're from. Get off my foot!

FORMER NAVY OFFICER now in business, late 30s, seeks sincere lady, late or early 20s. Ex-nuns or athletes given priority, any religion.

Irish Independent

For what lad can behold a pretty girl weeping for him without drying her ears on his breast.

Boston Globe

Close look at dating finds men choose attractive women

The Associated Press

LADY, 65, reasonable looks, medium build, 65, likes short walks, outings, the occasional drunk.

Westmorland Gazette

fly gets a girlfriend

Tim the Tiny Horse
was _tiny_.

He was so small that a pizza leaflet
would take him an hour and a half
to read...

So small was Tim that even
the small pizza was too big
for him.

What a waste of an
hour and a half.

slurp! slurp!

No. A typical lunch
for Tim the Tiny Horse
was a Hula Hoop
(preferably barbecue beef).

One day Tim's best friend Fly
announced that he had met
a lady fly and that she was
now his 'girlfriend'.

The upshot of this was that Fly
didn't want to see Tim as much.

On a couple of occasions
Tim went round
to see if Fly wanted
to come out to play,
only to find that

Fly's girlfriend was
already there.

'What does he want?'

'Perhaps she would like
to play too,'
said Tim the Tiny Horse,
hopefully.

'I think not!' said
Fly's new girlfriend,
looking at Tim in a
way that didn't make
him feel particularly
welcome.

Tail drooping

Head held low

Forlorn expression

Fly explained to Tim
[over the phone] that they
could still play together

but Tim should
give a little warning
before calling round.

A short time after that, Fly's
girlfriend decided she didn't
want to see Fly any more
(although they could still be
    friends).

There were no other
flies involved.

Whilst Tim was sorry to see Fly so upset...

he was secretly pleased that things were back to normal.

Tim felt a little bit guilty
about this feeling...

then he remembered
the look that Fly's
ex-girlfriend had given him...

and the feeling passed.

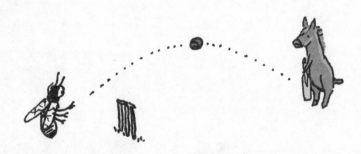

After all, you've got to stick by friends.

TRAVEL

Last week I flew on one of those new budget airlines. Before we took off, the stewardess reminded us to fasten our Sellotape.

This man sitting next to me pointed out of the window and said, 'Look at those people down there. They look like ants.'
And I said, 'They are ants. We haven't taken off yet!'

HARRY: I flew to New Zealand!
ALAN: Wow! Didn't that make your arms tired?

No matter how bad the in-flight movie, you still shouldn't walk out on it.

The ending was so predictable!

And the characterisations rather thin!

CONTROL TOWER: Please report your height and position.
PILOT: I'm 5 feet 11 and I'm in the cockpit.

Honolulu – it's got everything: sand for the children, sun for the wife, sharks for the wife's parents.

The resort was so dull, one day the tide went out and never came back.

Why did the mummy go on holiday?
To unwind.

What's a twack?
Something a twain runs on.

HARRY: Single to Portsmouth, please!
BOOKING CLERK: That'll be nine pounds fifty.
Change at Clapham Junction.
HARRY: I'll have my change here if you don't
mind!

An intercity train was travelling very slowly.
When it stopped suddenly a passenger asked
the conductor, 'Why have we stopped?' The
conductor said, 'There's a tortoise on the track.'
The passenger said, 'But we stopped for a
tortoise ten minutes ago.' The conductor
replied, 'I know – it caught up with us.'

What do you call a jelly in a 747?
A jet setter.

How do fleas travel?
By itch-hiking.

I was driving along with my nan and at every corner we went round she's going, 'Oh we're going too fast, slow down, we're going to crash!' I said, 'For pity's sake Nan — move over, I'll drive!'

I'm visiting a family of beavers in a lake in Holland.
Hamster dam?
No, Maastricht.

HARRY: Doctor, doctor, I keep on thinking I'm a ten-pound note.
DOCTOR: Try going on holiday – the change will do you good.

I knew a nymph who went to Calais.
Fairy?
No, Eurostar.

GRANDPA: I want to visit my daughter in Australia. How long would it take?
AIRLINE OPERATOR: Just a minute . . .
GRANDPA: That's great news. I'd like a return please!

Which hotel is green, wrinkly and rich in vitamin C?
The Savoy Cabbage Hotel.

SNOOTY HOTEL RECEPTIONIST: Do you have reservations?
HARRY: Plenty, but now we're here now and might as well stay.

HARRY: I'd like a return ticket, please.
BOOKING CLERK: Certainly, sir. Where to?
HARRY: Back here of course!

ANGUS: We took a trip from Scotland to sample the tourist attractions of England's capital.
HARRY: London Eye?
ANGUS: Aye, London, aye.

It was a terrible holiday camp. I went to the office and I said, 'It's about the roof of our chalet.'
The man said, 'What about it?'
And I said, 'We'd like one.'

He had the privilege also of viewing
a number of rare Egyptian tummies.

Cleveland (Ohio) paper

Dear Tourist,
Welcome to Jordan, the Holy Land, the loud of freasures and pleasures. We present to you this 'Touvist Guide' to help facilitate your stoy and we are glad to tell you how happy we are in your prescence.

Absent-minded Ray and Joyce Elkeron had a great time on a day trip – but haven't got a clue where they went! Now they have put an ad in the paper asking people if they recognise their description of the beauty spot.

It was only after they got home and planned a return trip that they realised they had no idea where they had been.

The Sun

'On my first day of Junior High I was in Geography class, and the teacher asked us if anybody knew the names of the continents. And I was sooo excited. I was like, Dammit! It's my first day of 7th grade, I'm in Junior High and I know this answer. So I raised my hand, I was the first one, and I said A-E-I-O-U!'

Jessica Simpson

A monkey trained to pick coconuts jumped on to a man passing a coconut tree in Kuala Lumpur. He mistook his head for a nut and tried to twist it off. The man was taken to hospital with a strained neck.

Sunday Mirror

I don't understand how the confusion arose!

'I've never really wanted to go to Japan. Simply because I don't like eating fish. And I know that's very popular out there in Africa.'

Britney Spears

Dear Sir,

With reference to our letter re Majorca tour, the flight you mention is completely booked, but we will inform you immediately someone falls out, as usually happens.

Fog and smog rolled over Los Angeles today, closing two airports and slowing snails to a traffic pace.

Los Angeles paper

tim and fly go out

Tim the Tiny Horse
was... well...
...very small.

To Tim a conker was a major
obstacle...

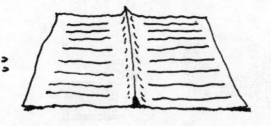

a crinkle in a piece of paper
was a real hurdle.

One day Tim and his friend
Fly decided to go to town.

They set off with Fly
riding on Tim's back.

'What an adventure!'
thought Tim the Tiny Horse.
'I could buy a chair!'

'And I could buy some
Shoes!' said Fly
out loud.

Then Tim remembered
that most chairs were
far too big for him...

...and Fly remembered that
most shoes come in sets of
2 rather than **6**.

'Is this trip entirely necessary?'
said Tim the Tiny Horse.
'After all, we don't really
need anything from town.'

'Yes,' said Fly, 'and the town
is an awfully long way.'

The answer was obvious:

With that they headed home.
This time it was Tim's turn to
ride on the back of Fly.

Sometimes you're
better off just staying
IN

FAMILIES

What happens when you see twin witches?
You find it difficult to tell which witch is which.

My parents hated me so much that they got another kid to play me in our home movies.

One day my parents challenged me to a game of hide-and-seek. Ten years later I found them in a town two hundred miles away.

HARRY: When I was a kid, I ran away from home. It took them six months to find me.
ALAN: Six months? Why?
HARRY: They didn't look.

My mum and dad never really got on – my mum was a Time Lord and my dad a Dalek.

I spent most of the day in the garden with my step ladder – not my real ladder, my step ladder.

My nan has got false teeth, so how can I believe a single word she says?

Did you hear about the invisible man who had children?
He couldn't find them.

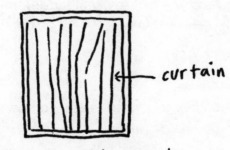

←— curtain

The Invisible Man's
Passport Photo

I come from a family of long livers. My dad had a liver three feet long.

liver ←

Gall bladder (size of a crisp
packet)
(Ready Salted) ←

My sister thinks I'm too nosy – at least, that's what she keeps writing in her diary.

TEACHER: Leon, I think your dad has been helping you with your homework.
LEON: No, sir – he did it all himself!

My family was made up of big eaters – after every meal we had to remember to count the children.

Why was the mummy glow-worm unhappy?
Because her children weren't very bright.

Help! —
Call your
Auntie!
I'm still
alive!

Regents Park

I have a stuffed tiger at home that reminds me of my uncle.
What's it stuffed with?
My uncle.

One day a man came to our door and said he was collecting for the children's home. So my dad gave him five of us.

I had a brother who was named after my father.
We called him Dad.

I wish...I hadn't fallen in!

A brother and sister were looking down a
wishing well. They both made a wish, and
waited expectantly. Suddenly, the sister lost her
footing and fell down the well.
'Amazing,' said the boy. 'It really works!'

Why don't you take your little brother to the zoo?
If they want him, they can come and get
him.

LEONA: I've got this ferret for my little brother.
JAMELIA: What a brilliant swap!

What powers your mum's
sister's space craft?
Auntie-matter.
How did she get it?
She won it in the NASA
summer fair tombola.
What is it called?
The STARSHIP AUNTY-PRIZE.

LEONA: My brother can do great bird imitations.
JAMELIA: You mean he can copy their voices?
LEONA: No – he eats worms.

FOR SALE: 83 Ford Grandad.

Wolverhampton Express and Star

'I owe a lot to my parents,
especially my mother
and father.'

Greg Norman

Let me out?!

'I was with Ian while he was at the club. He is not uncontrollable. He is big, but then boys are bigger than girls. None of the other mothers complained to me. Ian did shut Mrs Carter's little girl in a trunk. He's a naturally tidy child and puts all things away.'

Birmingham Post

He and his wife Gillian, who is a teacher, have three children, Gaven aged 13 and 11-year-old twins ugh and Helen.

Orpington News Shopper

Mrs Blackhouse, 37, and her two children, Harry, 10, and Sophie, 77, were on holiday last night.

Daily Express

Keeping all food under cover

is the first step towards ridding

the house of aunts.

Albany Journal

I am forwarding my marriage certificate and my 3 children, one of which was a mistake as you can see.

Letter to local government agency

Tim Gets His First Taste of Family Life

One day it was fly's birthday and Tim the Tiny Horse was invited round to Fly's for a birthday tea.

Fly was there, and his mum and Dad
and Fly's little sister.

Tim wished that he had a family – particularly a mummy.

(He did in fact have a cousin in Canada)

not a birthday cake – a hat!

maple leaves

Later on, an argument
broke out between Fly
and his sister...

which quickly turned
into a fight.

'I may not have a family,'
thought Tim, 'But at least
I don't have anyone shouting
that they hate me.'

Who could possibly
hate a tiny horse?

Fly explained later that that's
what <u>families</u> do sometimes.

Tim didn't really
believe him —

- he'd seen the look
in her eyes — she'd
meant it alright.

'You always hurt the one
you don't like that much,'
Thought Tim the Tiny Horse.

FOOD

Waiter, waiter – there's a fly in my soup!
Don't worry, sir – flies have very small
appetites.

The truth is I don't even like soup

How do ghosts like their eggs?
Terri-fried.

What does a hungry ghost have for tea?
Hunger-arian Ghoulash.

HARRY: Doctor, doctor, everyone says I'm crazy just because I love sausages.
DOCTOR: Of course you're not crazy – I like sausages too.
HARRY: Well, you must come and see my collection – I've got 2,000 of them!

ALAN: Waiter, is this all you have for dinner?
WAITER: No, sir – I'll be having a nice roast
when I get home.

ALAN: Waiter, call the manager. I can't eat this
terrible food.
WAITER: There's no point, sir. He won't eat it
either.

What does the astronaut
have for breakfast?
An unidentified frying
object.

What sort of sweets do
Martians eat?
Martian mallows.

How do you know when an
alien has been in your
fridge?
There's a note saying
'Sorry I used all the milk,
signed An Alien.'

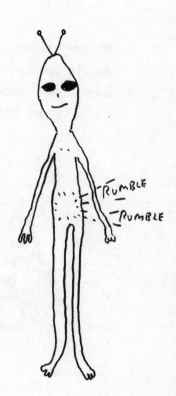

'We're going to have the chicken for dinner,'
said the farmer to his family.
'Cool,' said the youngest child. 'Can we
teach it to hold a knife and fork?'

HARRY: I want a sausage burnt on one side to a crisp but uncooked in the middle, some cold baked beans and a fried egg with rock-hard yolk topped with some really gristly bacon.
CAFÉ OWNER: But I can't cook a meal like that!
HARRY: Well, you did yesterday!

HARRY: The service in this restaurant is terrible!
ALAN: Yes, but the food is so bad I don't mind waiting!

What do you get if you cross roast pork with a telephone?
A lot of crackling on the line.

ALAN: I'll have a banana split made with two bananas, three scoops of vanilla ice cream, chocolate-chip sauce, chopped nuts and big dollop of whipped cream.
HARRY: Would you like a cherry on top?
ALAN: No thanks. I'm on a diet!

TEACHER: If I cut two apples and four pears in ten pieces what will I get?
ALAN: Fruit salad.

What do you call a man who's always dipping biscuits in his tea?
Duncan.

What did the frog order at McDonald's?
French flies and a Diet Croak.

I had a terrible row with my wife on Christmas morning. She said, 'You've done absolutely nothing to help with Christmas dinner!'
I said, 'What do you mean? Look at the turkey – I've plucked it and I've stuffed it. And all you've got to do now is kill it and put it in the oven!'

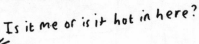
Is it me or is it hot in here?

ALAN: Waiter, waiter – how long will my chips be?
WAITER: About six centimetres each, I expect, sir.

Did you hear about the chef who got an electric shock?
He stood on a bun and a currant shot up his leg.

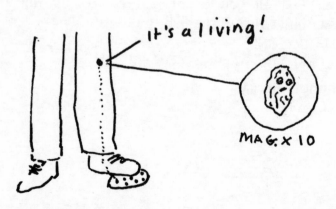

It's a living!

MAG. X 10

Why is there a line of plastic teen dolls waiting
for your Cajun chicken thighs?
It's a Barbie-queue.

Shall I tell you the joke about the butter?
I'd better not – you'll spread it around.

ALAN: I've caught a fish for supper.
HARRY: Brill!
ALAN: No, it's a haddock, but good eating
nonetheless.

HARRY: I keep thinking I'm a packet of biscuits.
PSYCHIATRIST: A packet of biscuits? You mean those little square ones with lots of little holes in them?
HARRY: That's right!
PSYCHIATRIST: You're not mad . . .
HARRY: Thank goodness!
PSYCHIATRIST: You're crackers!

I could murder some cheese

Why did the cookie cry?
'Cos her mother had been a wafer so long.

How do you make a cream puff?
Chase it round the garden.

How do you make a sausage roll?
Push it down a hill.

aw nothing
unhelpful bush

Cream Puff
cheers!

It went thataway!
helpful tree

man

Are you taking that lobster home for tea?
No, he's had his tea. Now I'm taking him
to the cinema.

FIRST HARICOT: How are you?
SECOND HARICOT: I've bean better.

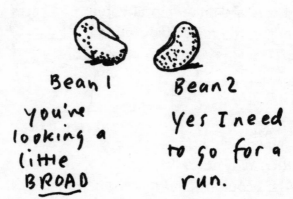

Bean 1
you're
looking a
little
BROAD

Bean 2
Yes I need
to go for a
run.

What do young Martians pick off their Christmas cake and discard?
Mars-ipan.

What is 200 feet tall, made of sponge cake, fruit, custard and whipped cream on top and stands in the middle of Paris?
The Trifle Tower.

ALAN: I made a rhubarb crumble three feet long.
HARRY: Why so big?
ALAN: I couldn't find any shorter rhubarb!

Why did the zombie get arrested for eating muesli?
They thought he was a cereal killer.

What do zombies like on their chops?
Grave-y.

What do Italian zombies eat?
Maggotty Bolognaise.

145

Which boy band is made of flour, butter, eggs and sugar?
Cake that.

you coming to Ascot this year?

Why do you think I'm wearing this ridiculous hat?

Why were the peas so wealthy?
They were minted.

What is the bravest food in the chip shop?
The pickled onion – because it is not a-fried.

Put that fork down and come back and fight like a man!

What's green, sits in a salad and sings 'Are you lonesome tonight?'
Elvis Parsley.

ERROR: The Observer wishes to apologise for a typesetting error in our *Tots and Toddlers* advertising feature last week which led to Binswood Nursery School being described as serving 'children casserole' instead of chicken casserole.

Leamington Spa Observer

One man was admitted to hospital
suffering from buns.

Bristol paper

I recommend my patients to eat
the tables with their meat, and
to be careful not to swallow their
food too quickly·

Medical Weekly

**AS FROM MONDAY,
THE CATERING ASSISTANTS
WILL SERVE CUSTOMERS
TO ALL POTATOES**

Factory noticeboard

Order chicken cut into serving pieces. Clean as necessary. Wash, drain, and blot on absorbent paper. Place chicken in deep bowl. Mash in a mortar the garlic, oregano, salt and peppercorns. Add to rum, mixed with soy sauce. Pour over children.

Ridgewood Record, New Jersey

I always scatter crumbs on the
waiter to attract the fish.

Angler's Mail

Mai Thai Finn is one of the students in the program and was in the center of the photo. We incorrectly listed her name as one of the items on the menu.

Community Life

For coping with unexpected guests, it is always a good plan to keep a few tons of sardines in the house.

Woman's Weekly

When you next have friends to dinner, one cut up in a mixed salad would be plenty for eight and a novel surprise for one's guests.

Woman's Weekly

SOME USEFUL INSTRUCTIONS

WARNING:
CONTAINS
NUTS

On a Sainsbury's peanut packet

Mr Ross's flab-fighting efforts, which reduced his 15-stone frame to two stone, won himself a buffet banquet for 80 and a portable colour television.

Harrogate Advertiser

tim does some cooking

Tim the Tiny Horse was by
no means a large horse...

but what he lacked
in the stature department
he more than made up for
in enthusiasm.

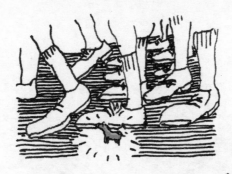

For instance, Tim was far too small to take part in the London Marathon...

[all those pounding feet would pose a real danger to him]

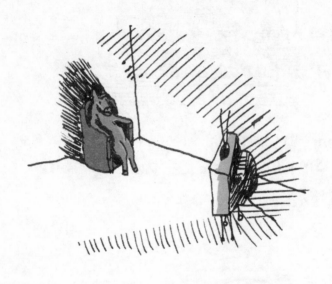

but that didn't stop him
enjoying it on the television.

One day, Tim the Tiny Horse
came upon the discarded wrapper
of a FUDGE BAR!

On closer inspection Tim realised that there was a list of ingredients.

'The fools!'
thought Tim the Tiny Horse.
'There's nothing to stop people
from making their own fudge bars!'

Back in his kitchen he set about
making his first fudge bar.

'Let's see what I need,' he said, reading the list of ingredients. 'Sugar... I've got that...'

'chocolate... I've got that ...'

'But what is 'non-hydrogenated vegetable fat'?'

'Hmmm,' he thought.

'Best leave it to the experts.'

And he ate the sugar...

And the chocolate...

and with a little imagination
it tasted a bit like
...fudge!

WEDDINGS

Leona insisted on getting married in her mother's wedding dress. She looked absolutely gorgeous – but her mum was freezing.

LEONA: I've just married the Queen's son. It was a nice wedding except the groom had an allergy to the salmon, and went all swollen and sweaty.
HARRY: Enlarged glossy prince?
LEONA: Yes, we'll be getting them back from Snappy Snaps any day.

Municipal Judge Charles S. Peery, who performed the brief wedding ceremony, said plaintively: 'I forgot to kill the bride. And I'm sorry.'

Tarrytown News

The three-tiered wedding cage had been made by the bride.

Somerset County Gazette

MR AND MRS SIMON PETERS

REQUEST THE HONOUR OF YOUR PRESENTS

AT THE MARRIAGE OF THEIR DAUGHTERS

EVE

TO

MR JAMES JOHNSON

Bride Of Two Mouths Sues Husband

**WEDDING DRESS
FOR SALE**

Worn once, by mistake

Best man was the bridegroom's brother, Mr Martin Gasson. A reception was held at Langford's Hotel, Hove, and the couple are honeymooning in grease.

Shoreham Herald

The bride wore a gown of sheer white lace with lace insects.

Cleveland newspaper

Traffic tailed back as far as Hemel Hempstead from the contra-flow system near the Berry Grove junction at Bushey where a bride is being re-painted at night and during the weekends.

Luton Evening Post-Echo

Tim's Best Friend's Wedding

After Tim had got over the initial shock of Fly's marriage plans—

(Fly had explained that because flies only tended to live about a year, in fact a week's courtship was perfectly respectable.

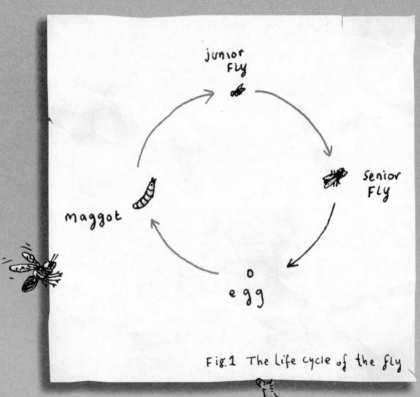

junior
FLY

Senior
Fly

maggot

egg

Fig.1 The life cycle of the fly

Plus he wasn't getting
any younger...

and you had to take
your opportunities where
you could.)

— Tim had some consolation from Fly asking him to be 'Best Horse'.

Tim took this as the ultimate endorsement of their friendship.

'What exactly does it entail?' said Tim the Tiny Horse.*

'There are various duties,' said Fly. 'But the main one is the Best Man's Speech!'

* He liked using the word tail in words.

Tim was so anxious at the thought

of this ...

that he staggered back ...

tripped on a

hundred and thousand ...

...and landed in
Fly's grandma's lap.

(Fly's grandma was now living
with Fly as she was unable to
cope on her own and was a risk
to herself from spiders.)

chair lift

Big hairy
spider

'A speech! Quelle horreur!'
he thought, lapsing into French.

'Yes, it should be funny too,'
said Fly. 'But keep it <u>clean</u>.'

On the way home he bought a book
called '101 Jokes For Your Best Man's
Speech' by someone called Barry Cryer.

'Funny name for
a comedian,'
thought Tim the
Tiny Horse.

As he read through it Tim realised
that whilst being very funny some
of the jokes were rather rude.

these two nuns so
how's that?
mother in
stop
she
get to bed
she
landed on his
see
anything like 6.

HO HO HE HA
HAHAHAHA
HA HA HA HEEHE
HEHE E HEEHO HO

Tim the Tiny Horse
laughed a lot...

but had a vision
of Fly's grandma

having a setback
if she ever heard them.

'You're on your own on this one,'
he thought to himself.

But he just couldn't think
of anything funny to say.

So he just wrote about why
he liked Fly and what
a good friend he was.

On the big day the speech went down a storm.

Many of the guests had tears in their eyes.

In fact it went down so well
that Tim decided to sling in one
of the jokes from the book...

(a particularly saucy one involving
an actress, a bishop... and a goat)

HA HA-OOPS!

and Fly's grandma laughed so hard
she fell off her chair.

BABIES

BABY 1: I don't think my mum is a very good mother.
BABY 2: Why's that?
BABY 1: 'Cos she keeps getting me up when I'm sleepy, and putting me to bed when I'm wide awake.

Why did the health 'n' safety officer have to measure the baby's biscuit?
He was doing a rusk assessment.

But, darling, this isn't our baby!
I know, but it's a much nicer pram!

What's the new baby's name?
I don't know. We can't understand a word
he says!

BLURBLE!

Funny name
for a Baby!

What is the baby fruit tree's favourite story?
'The Three Pears'.
How does it end?
They all lived appley every after.

PROUD FATHER: My new baby looks just
like me!
NURSE: Well, never mind. As long as it's healthy.

Why have you called your baby Zeus?
He is my 342nd child and it was the only
name left in the book.

HARRY: Here's my new daughter, doctor. You'll have noticed that she has a very long, narrow head and long sticky-out flat ears and a nose that looks like a propeller.
DOCTOR: Plain-looking child?
HARRY: Don't you start!

What do baby apes sleep in?
Apri-cots.

(Point to the centre of the palm of one of your hands. Explain to your friend that the spot you are pointing to is really a baby and that the baby is brand new and delicate and needs a lot of rest. Then say:)

Daddy says, 'Don't touch the baby!'
Mummy says, 'Don't touch the baby!'
Brother says, 'Don't touch the baby!'
Sister says, 'Don't touch the baby!'

(and each time point to the spot. Then ask your friend:)

'Where is the baby?'

(When he points to the spot or touches it, shout:)

'DON'T TOUCH THE BABY!'

Apparently the cause of ginger hair is if a mother during pregnancy eats too many Cheesy Wotsits.

Little tip for young mums: don't be tempted to take the baby into the bed – there's a chance you might roll onto the baby. And put your back out!

Was there anyone famous born on your
birthday?
No, only small babies.

How do astronauts get their baby to fall asleep?
They rocket.

In accordance with your instructions,
I have given birth to twins in the
enclosed envelope

State Population To Double By 2040; Babies To Blame

McClatchy News Service

Pasta Salad mixed with either chunks of fish or baby, barely cooked broad beans, then dressed with oil and vinegar, is very good, too.

Irish Times

Henry VIII by his own efforts increased
the population of England by 40,000.

Northern San Diego Shopper's Guide

207

DEAR MILKMAN,
BABY ARRIVED YESTERDAY,
PLEASE LEAVE ANOTHER ONE

Mr & Mrs Fly Get a New Addition

Tim the Tiny Horse noticed that Fly's new wife had put on a little weight...

and that her breath had
Started to smell of pickled
onions.

Well, you didn't have to be
Dr Robert Winston to work
out that this probably meant
that Fly's new wife was
going to have a MAGGOT.

'Indeed she is!'
beamed Fly, proudly.

'Congratulations!'
said Tim.

Although he <u>actually</u> thought
it was a little soon.

After all they'd only been
married a day and a half.

Tim hadn't even eaten his piece of wedding cake...

and the photos weren't even back from the printer's.

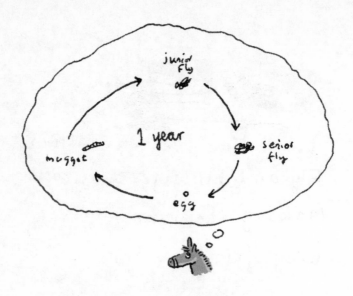

Then Tim remembered
the urgency of the fly's
life cycle...

and let it pass.

Fly and his wife set about
making their home more
baby friendly.

They installed a cot...

bought a number
of soft toys...

and even painted the walls of
the nursery with well-known
fly children's characters
such as...

Mickey Fly...

The
Telly-Flybbies...

and Flyddy
[the little fly...

with the red-and-yellow car].

In no time Fly's wife had
given birth to a baby
fly or 'Maggot'.

' He's got your nose! '
said Tim to Fly.

(closer)
(view)

{ much
{ closer view }
{ so you can
{ see his face }

Everyone stared at Maggot, who rolled around on his blanket ...

Grrrn!

and who made noises ...

Prrrrt!

from both ends.

Tim couldn't really see what this baby had to offer.

Then Maggot looked straight at Tim...

and <u>smiled</u>.

Tim smiled back.

Now he understood.

PETS AND OTHER ANIMALS

HARRY: Can you help me? I'm looking for a stray cat with one eye.
ALAN: Wouldn't it help if you used both eyes?

Which pet is sort of spiral shaped?
Helix the cat.

HARRY: Careful with that cat, it's worth £250!
ALAN: Gosh, how can a cat save so much money?

Where would you find a present for your cat's birthday?
In a cat-alogue.

ALAN: Doctor, doctor, I keep thinking I'm a cat.
DOCTOR: How long have you thought that?
ALAN: Ever since I was a kitten.

MUM: Why haven't you given the goldfish fresh water?
DAUGHTER: Because they haven't drunk the water I gave them yesterday.

I've been teaching my dog to beg. Last night he came home with 40p.

ALAN: I've got a miniature poodle.
HARRY: A miniature poodle?
ALAN: Yes, the miniature turn your back, he does a poodle.

My dog saw a seat in the park with a sign on it saying WET PAINT. So he did.

ALAN: I used to have a parrot once that laid
square eggs.
HARRY: Did it ever speak?
ALAN: Yes, it said, 'Ouch!'

I call my dog Isaiah.
Why?
Because one eye's 'igher than the other.

And the bad news is...
... I need glasses

↕ Height difference

ISIAH

I took my dog to a flea circus, and he stole the show.

ALAN: I'm going to buy a mongoose.
HARRY: Can you get one for me?
ALAN: I would but I don't know the right word
Is it 'mongooses'? Is it 'mongeese'? I don't want
to make a fool of myself.
HARRY: No problem. Just say, 'I'd like a
mongoose, please. And while you're at it, I'll
have another one.'

We called our dog 'Handyman' because he does
odd jobs around the house.

FIRST DOG: What's your name?
SECOND DOG: I'm not sure, but I think it's
'Down, boy'.

Just how intelligent are dolphins? Well, within just a few weeks of captivity they can train a human being to stand on the side of the pool throwing them fish at least three times a day.

HARRY: Our cat's gone missing!
POLICEMAN: Why don't you put a notice up in the park?
HARRY: Don't be silly, our cat can't read!

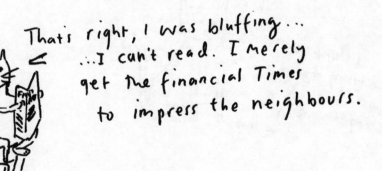

That's right, I was bluffing...
...I can't read. I merely get the financial Times to impress the neighbours.

ALAN: Mummy, Mummy, I fed the goldfish.
MUM: Yes, but I didn't mean feed him to
the cat.

Why couldn't the shepherdess see her dog?
She was collie-blind.

Alan went on holiday, leaving his cat with a neighbour. A few days later he phoned to ask how the cat was doing and the neighbour said, 'The cat fell off the roof and died.'

Alan was very upset and said to his neighbour, 'Couldn't you have broken it to me more gently? The first time I called you could have told me the cat was playing on the roof and fell off and wasn't looking too well, and then broken the bad news to me gradually over a couple of days.'

The neighbour apologised and hung up.

When Alan got home the neighbour rushed out to meet him looking concerned.

'Everything all right?' said Alan.

'How shall I put this, your mother was playing on the roof . . .'

ALAN: My dog bit my leg last night.
HARRY: Did you put anything on it?
ALAN: No, he liked it just as it was.

ALAN: My dog plays poker with me.
HARRY: That's fantastic! He must be very intelligent.
ALAN: Not really. Every time he gets a good hand, I can tell because he wags his tail.

I took my guinea pig to Cheddar Gorge.
Cavy?
That's an understatement!

CHEDDAR GORGE

I can't smell any cheese!

Did you hear about the blind grandfather who
went sky-diving?
He had a great time, but his
guide dog was terrified.

Commenting on a complaint from a Mr Arthur Purdey about a large gas bill, a spokesman for North West Gas said: 'We agree it was rather high for the time of year. It's possible Mr Purdey has been charged for the gas used up during the explosion that blew his house to pieces.'

Bangkok Post

DOG KENNEL, suit medium-sized dog. Good condition. Very turdy. Buyer collects. £9.99.

Wisbech Standard

1 GOLDEN LABRADOR Dog for sale,
2 years old, good driver, clean licence.

Hampshire paper

ROAD CONDITIONS in the New
Forest were the worst known for years.
In several places the roads were lined
with cats unable to climb
the snow-covered
hills.

Sussex paper

WANTED – Man to take care of cow that does not smoke or drink.

Pickens Sentinel

Personal Profile: A Netherlandphile with two grown children, a cat who snores, a Labrador with eczema and a passion for perfection.

At a lunch hour assembly at the school, Mrs Thomson gave an interesting talk, with slides, on Baboo, her pet baboon. She said that, although some people were scared by such a large animal, she felt completely at home with him, having spent fifteen years in Africa with her husband.

School newsletter

Police chased the getaway cat for more than 40 miles.

Daily Mail

A VISUALLY IMPAIRED San Francisco man argued he wasn't driving solo in the commuter lane reserved for cars carrying two or more people because his dog, Queenie, was helping him navigate.

Seattle Times

tim
gets a pet

With Fly now a family man...

Tim found that he had a bit
more time on his hands.

And when there was nothing
on the box he would feel...

bored ...

Or worse — lonely.

[but never sorry for himself —
he was just putting that
sad face on for the picture.]

One bank holiday monday, whilst taking a stroll he saw a man walking his dog.

'Humans have pets for company!' he thought.

'That is exactly what I should do!'

... and he headed off
to the pet shop.

Unfortunately all the pets in the shop were rather too big. Some of them were downright frightening.

GRRrrr!

RARRrr!

Especially the dogs.

Even the hamsters were
the size of elephants to
Tim the Tiny Horse.

'Ho·Hum,' thought Tim the Tiny Horse.

'It looks like I must settle
for a life on my own.'

Just then, he spotted a greenfly
snacking on the stem of a flower.

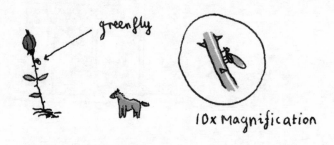

greenfly

10x Magnification

Tim got chatting to the greenfly
(who didn't seem to be that bright).

vacant-looking eyes

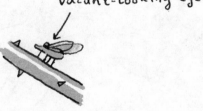

'I don't suppose you'd be my pet?'
asked Tim the Tiny Horse.

'sure, why not?' said the
greenfly.

'Great!' said Tim.
'What's your name?'

'George!'
said the greenfly.

And with that, using a piece
of cotton as a lead, Tim
took his new pet home.

HOUSE AND HOME

How could the harbour master lift up his home? It was a light house.

I'm not saying the place was messy, but last week some vandals broke in and tidied up.

Our house was such a mess when I was a kid
that I used to wipe my feet before going out!

The dust was so thick on the floor that the
cockroaches were going round on stilts.

Look at the muck in here!

Is your house in this street?
Yes.
Better hurry up and move it! There's a car coming!

An idiot heard that most accidents take place in the home. So he moved.

ALAN: Is your new settee comfy, Harry?
HARRY (*nodding*): Sofa, so good.

I hope you don't mind me asking, but why are
you erecting a barrier round your house?
To prevent flooding.
Noah Fence?
None taken, mate.

I think my bathroom is haunted. I keep hearing weird knocking noises and the sink doesn't seem to fill up properly.
Strange taps?
Exactly!

The walls were so thin, the neighbours were dipping their bread in our gravy.

Did you hear about the flea who won the
lottery?
He bought a dog in Spain.

We were all great singers in our house.
We had to be.
Why?
There was no lock on the lavatory door.

ALAN: Bet I can jump higher than a house.
HARRY: Bet you can't.
ALAN: I win. Houses can't jump.

Why is it only Tudor buildings that we mock?

Birds Eye recently gave a banquet at which the Minister of Housing was guest of honor pre-cooked, frozen and re-heated on site.

Catering Management

Nothing brightens the garden in spring more than primrose pants.

Weekly paper

DOVER ROAD
Semi-det. house with
sea through lounge.

Folkestone, Hythe and District Herald

A spacious 3 bed semi-detached property comprising 3 god sized bedrooms and a large loving room.

Leamington Spa Courier

WOMAN WANTED, to share Fat with another.

MALE (24) seeks doom in central flat.
Please phone . . .

Edinburgh Evening News

Peaceful, relaxing, self-contained, stone built cottages and bungalows. Sandy beach only 300 years away.

Wales Holidays 1983 brochure

... a substantial well-built semi ...
3 bedrooms ... garden areas to front
and rear with fish pong.

Stockport Express

A detached 213 bedroom
bungalow on large corner plot.

South Wales Echo

FOR RENT: 6-room hated apartment.

FOR SALE:
A rarely comfortable modern detached residence.

Irish Times

tim gets
all capitalist
on us

Tim the Tiny Horse had never
had much in the way of
material goods.

So imagine his excitement when he received a cheque for a considerable sum of money from sales of his book.

'I should be careful with this money,' thought Tim the Tiny Horse.

'This sort of luck
doesn't come along
every day...'

'I should invest it...

...in a buy-to-let flat!'

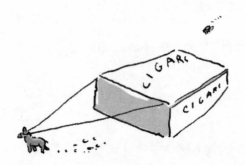

He went straight out and bought
himself an empty cigar box...

and set about converting it
into a 'Loft-style' apartment.

He'd learnt from the TV
that it was important to
keep things neutral.

So he painted the inside
of the box with
Tipp-Ex.

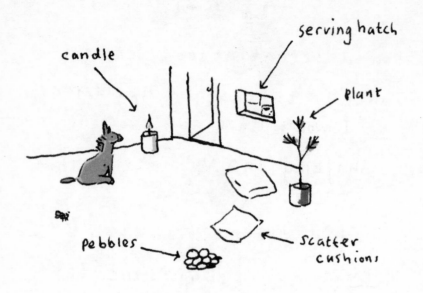

candle

serving hatch

plant

pebbles

scatter cushions

As he surveyed his handiwork he could almost hear the light, jazz-funk music that they always play over the post-makeover footage.

'I won't have any problem shifting this,' he thought.

Within a couple of days a ladybird turned up; it seemed her own house had burnt down.

'Is that a greenfly?'
said the ladybird,
looking at George...

and licking her lips.

'Yes, but you wouldn't
want to eat him... he's ill,'
lied Tim. 'Listen, take
the flat rent-free until
you're back on your feet,'
he said, taking pity on
the ladybird.

So, not only had he spent a lot of money on the refurb [Tipp-Ex isn't cheap, you know] ...

he now wasn't getting any money in to cover his costs.

A couple of weeks later
Tim the Tiny Horse received
a complaint from the
neighbours ...

that the ladybird had had
rather too many guests...

many of whom
had stayed overnight.

When he went to visit
the property...

he found fifteen
juvenile ants living there!

Inside there was utter chaos!

upturned
candle

ant in
serving
hatch

dead
plant

Stray pebbles

scatter cushions
half eaten

It seemed that the Ladybird
had sub-let it.

'What a nice way
to repay kindness!'
thought Tim the Tiny Horse.

With the help of Fly and a trail of
sugar, Tim managed to get the
ants to leave his cigar-box
apartment.

Tim's experiences in the property
market had been something of
a _let-down_.

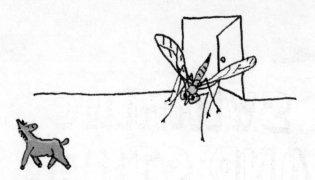

So he flogged the flat to
a daddy long legs.

Sometimes it's just nice to
know your money's safe.

SWIMMING AND OTHER THINGS TO DO IN THE WATER

On what did Tarzan cross the river?
A gi-raft.

I went swimming with a dolphin but it didn't turn out how I hoped. It got caught in the turnstile.

I thought I could trust the people who use my pool, but all I know is that when I filled it last year I put in 10,000 gallons and when I emptied it last week I took out 11,000 gallons.

HARRY: I'm going swimming after my lunch.
ALAN: Really? I'm getting mine from the canteen.

My little brother was banned from our local leisure centre for weeing in the swimming pool. I told them lots of little boys wee in the swimming pool.
They said, 'Yes, but not from the high-diving board.'

ALAN: I've just been pinched rotten whilst paddling near yonder breakwater.
HARRY: Crabby?
ALAN: Yes, I am now in a very bad mood.

ALAN: Mum, come quick! Dad waded out to sea
and now he's up to his ankles in the water!
MUM: That's not very dangerous.
ALAN: It is when he's upside down.

...Blurble-help-
...Blurble!

HUSBAND: I hate to say this, but your swimming costume is very tight and very revealing.
WIFE: Wear your own one, then.

Which detergent powder did the Beach Boys use to wash their Hawaiian shirts?
Surf.

ALAN: Dad, I'm afraid the car's got water in the carburettor.
HARRY: Where *is* the car?
ALAN: In the lake.

What do you call a man who doesn't sink?
Bob.

ALAN: What time shall we meet at the leisure centre?
HARRY: Tennish?
ALAN: Actually I fancy a swim.

Ah, There's been some confusion....

INFLATABLE RUBBER DINGHY FOR SALE

Good as new apart from slight puncture. £25

The announcement of the disqualification
was greeted by booze from spectators at
the pool.

Gloucestershire Echo

During the Moscow Olympics of 1980 an athlete from Guinea Bissau refused to take part in the 3,000 metres steeplechase event. When asked why he would not run he explained that it was the water jump which 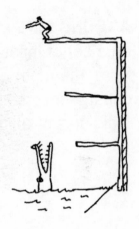 worried him. You just don't jump into water in Guinea Bissau: there might be crocodiles.

From Steven Winkworth, Famous Sporting Fiascos

A YOUNG GIRL who was blown out to sea on a set of inflatable teeth was rescued by a man on an inflatable lobster. A coastguard spokesman commented, 'This sort of thing is all too common.'

The Times

The seaman, severely injured when the ship was three hours out, was taken to hospital and the hippopotamus removed.

Daily Telegraph

HEALTH OFFICIALS: POOLS, DIARRHEA NOT GOOD MIX

World Herald

tim gets wet

One day Tim threw a particularly juicy stick for George...

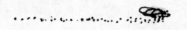 

which landed in a puddle.

But instead of stopping at
the water's edge...

George dived into the puddle

and disappeared under the water.

Tim waited for George to re-surface...

but there was no sign
of the little greenfly

except for one bubble.

Tim suddenly remembered
that on the whole greenflies
can't swim

(as anyone who drinks tea will tell you).

Quick as a flash Tim took off
his shoes...

and dived into the puddle.

It was a very deep puddle.

HELP!

Tim splashed about gasping
for air...

Then he remembered that
he couldn't swim either!

Under the water he went...

then he managed to grab at
a length of cotton floating on
the water's surface.

As he took hold of the cotton
he found he was being dragged
to shore.

where he found that the piece
of cotton was being pulled by
George the Greenfly.

'You're a bit wet!'
said George.

'Hm!' said Tim the Tiny Horse.

CELEBRITIES

ALAN: I'm ashamed to be seen with that Prince William these days.
HARRY: Ridiculous heir?
ALAN: Yes I really think he should just shave it off and be done with it.

What does Prince Philip wear on his hernia?
The National Truss.

Why did the Queen buy her husband a new throne?
To chair him up.

What other sport is there where you only wear <u>shorts</u> and <u>Gloves</u>?

I used to be a boxer. I fought Amir Khan once. In the first round, I really had him worried. He thought he'd killed me.

How often does Keira practise acting?
Nightly.

HARRY: I recently went to see an open-air
performance of *Romeo and Juliet* in the winter
and sitting in front of me were that band who
had a hits with 'Yellow' and 'Trouble'.
ALAN: Coldplay?
HARRY: Freezing, and a very sad ending too.

What's pink with yellow spots and big eyes and
sings, 'I'm lovin' angels instead'?
Mr Blobby Williams.

I will not be joining
Cake That for the
← reunion!

Which attractively shy film star has been
awarded a bursary to study adhesives?
Glue Grant.

HARRY: What do you call a kebab that froths at
the mouth and sings 'I'm hung up on you'?
ALAN: A Mad-Donna.

What was Bruce Lee's favourite dinner?
Karate chops.

I've just dressed the wounds of the Rolling
Stones.
Bandage?
About 357 years if you add them all up.

Why is the Queen 30 cm tall?
She is a ruler.

How does the Conservative Party record their meetings?
They have Da vid Camera on.

I went for an Indian with a supermodel, but the lentils tasted of washing-up liquid.
Soapy Dahl?
No, it was Naomi Campbell.

How did Scary Spice demand attention from her pet seabird?
If you want to be my Plover, you must be my friend!

Which TV presenter lies around on the boat all day?
Dec.

My wife thinks she's the Queen of England.
Have you ever told her she isn't?
What, and blow my chances of a knighthood!

ALAN: Aarrgh! Look at the state of my hair!
HAIRDRESSER: But you said you wanted it cut
like David Beckham's.
ALAN: Yes, but David Beckham doesn't have his
hair cut like this!
HAIRDRESSER: He does if he comes here.

Which TV presenter lives in a labyrinthine
underground nest?
Ant.

Germany v Spain: Psychic Octopus Paul Unfazed By Death Threats, Says Keeper

Hey! It's the price of fame!

'As with every young player, he's only 18.'

Sir Alex Ferguson, talking about a young David Beckham

'I was in a no-win situation, so I'm
glad that I won rather than lost.'

Frank Bruno

'That's just the tip of the ice cube'

Ex-MP Neil Hamilton

'I have opinions of my own –
strong opinions – but I don't
always agree with them.'

George W. Bush

'Beyond its entertainment value,
Baywatch has enriched and, in so
many cases, helped save lives.'

David Hasselhoff

Hi I'm The Hoff

'I don't know much about football. I know what a goal is, which is surely the main thing about football.'

Victoria Beckham

tim thinks about selling out

Tim

a Tic-Tac

Tim the Tiny Horse was <u>tiny</u>.

BORDERSTONES

Tim the Tiny
Horse
signing today

but since he was now a published
author he was in demand.

why, he'd even been interviewed by
top TV presenter Mariella Frostrup.

He tried not to let this extra
attention go to his head.

but if he was honest...
every now and then...

wazzup?

it did. For instance...

Once he'd been waiting so long
at the Deli counter in the
supermarket...

that he bellowed at the top of
his voice:

DO YOU KNOW WHO I AM!?!

Fortunately, no one could hear him (because he was so small)

Tim now bought his olives on the internet.

One day Tim had a phone call
from a lady asking if he'd
like to be in an advert

'Absolutely not!' Thought
Tim the Tiny Horse

'I would never compromise
my artistic integrity

by saying something I didn't
mean, for money!'

Then the lady told him
the fee.

'Send the script over
and I'll think about it,'
said Tim, hedging his bets.

Unfortunately the advert
was for FLY SPRAY.

Which put Tim in a rather tricky predicament.

Should he promote something that might well be used to kill his best friend and his pet?*

/ SLAM!

No contest. He turned the advert down.

*A problem peculiar to those who consort with insects.

Imagine his disgust when 2 months later he caught the same advert on TV featuring

His arch-enemy the <u>ladybird</u> in a blue horse costume.

It was becoming clear that
ladybirds had absolutely
no sense of fair play.